Anyone embarking on a new leadership opportunity is an emerging leader. Contact Eddie Turner Jr. via email at eddie@eddieturnerllc.com. Mention: "Emerging Leaders" in the email subject line to receive a free twenty-minute, no-obligation consultation.

140 Simple Messages to Guide Emerging Leaders

140 Actionable Leadership Messages for
Emerging Leaders and Leaders in Transition

Eddie Turner Jr.

An Actionable Business Journal

E-mail: info@thinkaha.com
20660 Stevens Creek Blvd., Suite 210
Cupertino, CA 95014

Published by THiNKaha®
20660 Stevens Creek Blvd., Suite 210, Cupertino, CA 95014
http://thinkaha.com
E-mail: **info@thinkaha.com**

First Printing: September 2018
Hardcover ISBN: 978-1-61699-269-9   1-61699-269-7
Paperback ISBN: 978-1-61699-268-2   1-61699-268-9
eBook ISBN: 978-1-61699-270-5   1-61699-270-0
Place of Publication: Silicon Valley, California, USA
Paperback Library of Congress Number: 2018947689

Trademarks

All terms mentioned in this book that are known to be trademarks or service marks have been appropriately capitalized. Neither THiNKaha, nor any of its imprints, can attest to the accuracy of this information. Use of a term in this book should not be regarded as affecting the validity of any trademark or service mark.

Warning and Disclaimer

Every effort has been made to make this book as complete and as accurate as possible. The information provided is on an "as is" basis. The author(s), publisher, and their agents assume no responsibility for errors or omissions. Nor do they assume liability or responsibility to any person or entity with respect to any loss or damages arising from the use of information contained herein.

Acknowledgments

I am incredibly grateful to my amazing wife, Ashlea Turner, who is my best friend and confidant. Her love and encouragement help me to accomplish my goals and thrive.

I am appreciative of my father for teaching me discipline and independence. I want to acknowledge my sister, Monica Turner, a woman who has always been precocious and shown tremendous leadership.

Thank you to my numerous uncles, aunts, cousins and my brother, Brian Turner. All of you have played a role in my success through your examples and support.

To my nephew, Braylon Burns, an emerging leader, I hope these short messages guide you to become the best leader you can be.

Special thanks to Sylvie di Giusto, Phil M. Jones, Mitchell Levy, Anna Liotta, Jenilee Maniti, Cathi Jo McGee, J. R. Phillips, Dr. Laura Sicola, Greg Williams, and Carl Winchester for your insights and inspiration through this process.

There are many people who formed the core building blocks of my life and spirituality from an early age. You taught me a way of life and truth that made me who I am. I may not see you as often anymore, but your examples of leadership and the life lessons you taught me as an emerging leader are indelibly etched in my mind and heart.

There are countless mentors, professors, teachers, friends, and colleagues to whom I owe a debt of gratitude for helping craft my view of leadership. Some of these people I have known all my life, others I've only come to know the last couple of years. I dare not start a list for fear of leaving someone out. I have tremendous love and appreciation for you all.

I must say a special thank you to the members of the National Speakers Association (NSA). The National Speakers Association has had the biggest impact on me as a professional and is the reason writing a book became a goal for me. I have learned so much about entrepreneurship, marketing, speaking, and running a business from this incredible organization.

I am also deeply appreciative for the Association for Talent Development (ATD). In the Association for Talent Development, I have had a chance to develop and grow as a leader. I have had the chance to work with chapters around the country and speak and teach internationally. I value my membership and relationships in the ATD community.

Thank you to my fellow Board members at the International Institute for Facilitation (INIFAC). I value the role you have allowed me to serve in on the Board as we spread the power of facilitation across the globe.

Dedication

This book is dedicated to my mother, Barbara Turner. I owe my mother the world. She is my rock and has always been there for me and supported me no matter what. There is truly nothing like a mother's love, and Barbara Turner is the epitome of all that a loving mother should be.

How to Read a THiNKaha® Book
A Note from the Publisher

The AHAthat/THiNKaha series is the CliffsNotes of the twenty-first century. These books are contextual in nature. Although the actual words won't change, their meaning will every time you read one, as your context will change. Be ready: you will experience your own AHA moments as you read the AHA messages™ in this book. They are designed to be standalone actionable messages that will help you think about a project you're working on—an event, a sales deal, a personal issue, etc.—differently. As you read this book, please think about the following:

1. It should only take fifteen to twenty minutes to read this book the first time. When you're reading, write in the underlined area one to three action items that resonate with you.
2. Mark your calendar to re-read this book again in thirty days.
3. Repeat step one, and mark one to three more AHA messages™ that resonate. They will most likely be different than the first time. By the way, this is also a great time to reflect on the AHA messages™ that resonated with you during your last reading.

After reading a THiNKaha book, marking your AHA messages™, re-reading it, and marking more AHA messages™, you'll begin to see how these books contextually apply to you. AHAthat/THiNKaha books advocate for continuous, lifelong learning. They will help you transform your AHAs into actionable items with tangible results, until you no longer have to say AHA to these moments—they'll become part of your daily practice as you continue to grow and learn.

Mitchell Levy, The AHA Guy at AHAthat
publisher@thinkaha.com

Contents

Introduction

When I decided to complete my undergraduate degree as an adult, I was in my early thirties. I matriculated at Northwestern University to formally study leadership and organization behavior. Having already worked for Quaker Oats (now Pepsi), Xerox, and General Electric, corporations *Forbes* magazine calls the "most admired companies," I felt I already understood leadership. I had seen the best of the best leading the world's best. At Northwestern University, I learned more about leadership than I ever imagined.

I was immersed in a level of empirical research and academic rigor I had not anticipated. I was introduced to new leadership theories and the latest scholarly research available at the time. With this new knowledge, I began to look at what I thought I knew about leadership through a different lens. I began to analyze leadership successes and failures in my own life and those around me. I worked hard to learn from those lessons and I recalibrated my own leadership style.

After leaving Northwestern University, I continued my growth and development as a leader. I have gained a level of expertise in the exercise of leadership and the development of leadership capacity in oneself and others. I am now an International Certified Coach™ and an Emotional Intelligence (EQ-i 2.0 and EQ-i 360) practitioner. I have also completed the "Art and Practice of Leadership Development" executive education program at the John F. Kennedy School of Government at Harvard University.

Leadership is one of the world's oldest professions. There are countless resources for one to learn about leadership and do in-depth study. In this book, my goal is not to provide a scholarly tome, but rather to provide emerging leaders short messages for guidance and success. I do this through 140 short messages that have helped me navigate life.

Why am I providing 140 messages, some have asked? Why not use traditional numbers, like five, ten, or 100? We are living at a time when Twitter and its 140-character limitation (now 280) is being used by leaders in all areas of life and at all levels of organizations. Some leaders are exemplary in their use of Twitter and others less so. My goal is to leverage the zeitgeist we are living in to show how by using the limited characters allowed by Twitter, leaders can communicate strong messages that make a positive impact on people's lives. For that reason, this actionable leadership journal contains 140 Twitter-length, easy-to-share messages written as a guide for emerging leaders on living, learning, and developing themselves and others on their journey to success.

Additionally, I have become convinced of the power of well-crafted short messages for another reason. I was a *Forbes* contributor for a year. As a member of the Forbes Coaches Council during that year, I contributed to thirty question-and-answer columns. The answers to the Q&As I submitted to *Forbes* were required to be 400 characters or fewer. This is slightly longer than Twitter's new 280-character limit. Some of the columns I appeared in were read by as few as 2,000 people. The most popular columns I contributed to were read by more than 30,000 people. This clearly shows that people found value in our succinct messages and shared them with others. Hence, I believe there is value in the messages contained in this book designed to be an actionable leadership journal.

As I sat down and began to write, it was enlightening to me to see just how many stories, phrases, and quotes I use in my coaching practice, professional speeches, and in simple everyday conversations that have become part of me but originated with people in my life. From my perspective, this shows the impact of these messages. I share these simple messages as a guide for emerging leaders on their journey to success, as well as for those emerging leaders who have already achieved success but refuse to get complacent and therefore, continue looking for new ways to emerge as a leader!

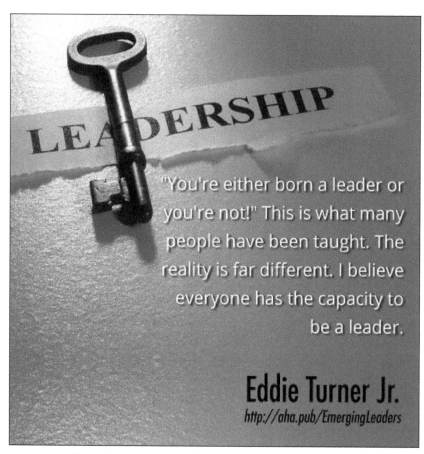

"You're either born a leader or you're not!" This is what many people have been taught. The reality is far different. I believe everyone has the capacity to be a leader.

Eddie Turner Jr.
http://aha.pub/EmergingLeaders

Share the AHA messages from this book socially by going to
http://aha.pub/EmergingLeaders.

Section I

Leadership Begins in Youth

Children are great imitators. They learn how to talk not by reading books or sitting in a training course but by watching their parents and family members. Similar to learning a language and speaking their first words, life's earliest lessons are learned by children from their parents. Later, other adult influences play a role in how young people define and begin to express leadership.

As you read this section, consider your own leadership lessons. Who were your first role models and leadership influences? How have they changed over time? How have they stayed the same?

Leadership lessons and experience begin in youth. Experienced leaders should never underestimate the power they can have on an emerging leader's life by teaching and modeling leadership lessons for them at an early age and by taking specific actions to develop their leadership capacity.

1

Please read and share these "140 Simple Messages to Guide Emerging Leaders."
http://aha.pub/EmergingLeaders

_____

_____

_____

2

This book of simple messages is a guide for emerging leaders on their journey to success. These messages have worked for me, and I believe they can work for you!

_____

_____

_____

3

"I work with leaders to accelerate performance and
drive impact!"™
—Eddie Turner

4

You're either born a leader or you're not!
This is what many people have been taught.
The reality is far different.
I believe everyone has the capacity to be a leader.

5

Some people are natural-born leaders. Was it nature or nurtured? This is the subject of much research. Leadership is an art and a skill, and it CAN be learned.

_____

_____

_____

6

My dad always taught me to be a leader, not a follower. Many years later, I learned a leader can, in fact, be both!

_____

_____

_____

7

My mother played the first role in my leadership development. She read to me every night as a child because she believed readers become leaders. What are you reading?

_____

_____

_____

8

My dad taught me to always be twice as good as my competition. He said it was never acceptable to be "good enough" or "just as good."

_____

_____

_____

9

My uncles and aunts had strong work ethics. They learned the value of hard work from my grandparents and reinforced those messages in the next generation of our family. They always said: "Work hard! Don't take it easy. Hard work pays off!"

_____

_____

_____

10

Nothing will work unless you do. —Maya Angelou

_____

_____

_____

11

My father and uncles were the first people to teach me the importance of visual leadership. They taught me the importance of a good suit and shined shoes in presenting myself as a professional.
How do you show visual leadership?

_____

_____

_____

12

"Don't preach me a sermon, show me one!" I heard this from a minister when I was young and never forgot it. To live as a leader means to "practice what we preach." Be a model of exemplary behavior at all times!

_____

_____

_____

13

My dad used to say to me: "Don't learn how to use a computer, learn how to build one." He wanted me to be ahead of the curve and always ready for change. Leaders look out across the horizon and not just at what is right in front of them.

_____

_____

_____

14

"Stay ready so you don't have to get ready!" A colleague from school always said this. This is a different version of my father's words on being ahead of the curve and always ready for change. I live by these words.

_____

_____

_____

15

When opportunity comes, it is too late to prepare.
—John Wooden

_____

_____

_____

16

There are no secrets to success. It is the result of
preparation, hard work, and learning from failure.
—Colin Powell

_____

_____

_____

17

Experience is not always the best teacher! You don't have to put your hand on the stove to know it's hot. Reading, observation, and reflection provide tremendous learning for leaders.

_____

_____

_____

18

"People are never as serious as when they are laughing or joking."
—Michael Bernard Thomas
Great leaders understand the power of their words and don't hide behind comedy.

_____

_____

_____

19

To keep us humble and provide a reality check, my great-grandmother always said: "Keep on living!" Time and maturity teach us to appreciate things we took for granted when younger.

_____

_____

_____

20

Have doubts or think you can't succeed? My great-grandmother always said: "Nothing beats a failure but a try!" I've learned that great leaders gain experience through trial and error.

_____

_____

_____

21

Nothing raises the price of a blessing as its removal!
—Paul Illingworth
Great leaders recognize the cost of short-sighted
thinking and learn to be circumspect when
making decisions.

_____

_____

_____

22

"Sometimes you have to EXPECT the worse,
and ACCEPT the best!"
Advice to avoid disappointment.

_____

_____

_____

23

I've learned that people will forget what you said, people will forget what you did, but people will never forget how you made them feel. —Maya Angelou
How do you make people feel?

_____

_____

_____

24

When an old man dies, a library burns.
—African Proverb
My first history books were my grandparents.
Cherish and learn leadership lessons
from your elders while you can.

_____

_____

_____

25

Many people saw leadership potential in me that was seeded by my parents. They played a role in cultivating the seed that allowed me to blossom into the leader I am today. What young person can you begin to help cultivate leadership capacity?

_____

_____

_____

26

Leadership begins in youth! Paper routes, doing chores around the home, or getting involved in religious or civic organizations early in life helps build discipline and character, which provide a solid foundation for leadership.

_____

_____

_____

Learn how to handle conflict early in your career, and it will hold you in good stead. Poor conflict resolution skills can permanently derail leaders.

Eddie Turner Jr.
http://aha.pub/EmergingLeaders

Share the AHA messages from this book socially by going to
http://aha.pub/EmergingLeaders.

Section II

Early Career Leadership

An emerging leader's first jobs significantly influence their view of leadership. The first jobs in teenage years, during the college years, and the first few post-collegiate professional jobs create a lasting impression of what leadership is and how it should be exercised. Many emerging leaders imitate what they experienced in these contexts, assuming this is the way leadership works and what it takes to be successful. This underscores the importance of experienced leaders setting a good example of leadership and modeling excellence. Where good examples are not readily available, emerging leaders should look outside their workplace and immediate sphere of influence to find role models who demonstrate leadership excellence.

Emerging leaders do well to find a mentor early in their career to help guide them properly instead of leaving their leadership development to chance. Having a strong mentor will also assist in taking ownership of one's career and work to control the navigation and trajectory on their own, rather than wait for someone else—which may never happen or may push them in a direction less than optimal for them.

Many things in life are impacted by an early start or an early diagnosis. Start your career off right! Take inventory of where you are today. If your career has gotten off to a slow start or one that is less than ideal, change it now. It is never too late to become the emerging leader you are destined to be!

27

There is a difference between your VOCATION and your AVOCATION. One is your job, the other is your hobby. There is great joy when your avocation can be your vocation!

_____

_____

_____

28

I've been fortunate to always do what I love: work in technology and help people through the power of communication, coaching, teaching, and facilitation. Find your passion as a leader.

29

I have been a teacher as early as I can remember and a speaker since I was 12. One of my biggest epiphanies was when my manager told me:
"You TRAIN dogs, you TEACH people."

_____

_____

_____

30

Facilitation is the leadership skill of the future.
Become a facilitative leader!

_____

_____

_____

31

The most effective teachers and trainers facilitate to educate! Are you effective?

_____

_____

_____

32

Sitting is the new smoking!—Harvard Business Review Healthy leaders are active. Are you?

_____

_____

_____

33

Look for stretch assignments early in your career. Challenge yourself rather than get comfortable or complacent. You must actively grow your skills, or without even realizing it, they will atrophy.

_____

_____

_____

34

One point is a datum. Two points define a line.
Three points are a trend.
—J. R. Phillips
Facts and stats matter! Effective leaders analyze trends when making decisions.

_____

_____

_____

35

Are you watching the trends of your profession? When is the last time you studied the data for your industry? Technology is the great disrupter. Are you keeping up?

_____

_____

_____

36

Learn how to handle conflict early in your career, and it will hold you in good stead. Poor conflict resolution skills can permanently derail leaders.

_____

_____

_____

37

Turn loose, forgive, move on! —J. R. Phillips
Simple yet powerful advice for conflict resolution.

_____

_____

_____

38

You can't be the world's best-kept secret!
—Tim Durkin

_____

_____

_____

39

Be known for being an expert at something and build a reputation for excellence! Share your expertise in forums internal and external to your company and through short elevator pitches to increase your visibility.

_____

_____

_____

40

"Dress for the job you want, not the job you have!"
—Diane Yavor
Do you dress for success?

_____

_____

_____

41

To be qualified, you must be certified.
—J. R. Phillips
What professional certification(s) do you hold?

_____

_____

_____

42

Don't let your undergraduate degree be the last time you invest in yourself. Invest in a new credential or learning experience every year. Like financial investments, this pays bigger dividends the earlier you start.

_____

_____

_____

43

Successful leaders learn how to manage their time. "Getting Things Done (GTD)" by David Allen is one of my favorite methodologies for time management. What time management strategy do you use?

_____

_____

_____

44

"All calendar items are not created equal!"
—Bob Dean
Leaders need to be flexible. At times, this means recalibrating priorities and the demands on your time.

_____

_____

_____

45

My grandfather had a 3rd grade education, but he is one of the smartest men I've ever known. Why? Because he had COMMON SENSE. Academic achievement is not the only measurement of knowledge and intellect.

_____

_____

_____

46

When someone shows you who they are, believe them the first time. —Maya Angelou

_____

_____

_____

47

Early in our careers, it is easy to think we know everything and others are not as sharp as us. Resist that thinking! Great leaders understand they don't know what they don't know, and therefore, keep an open mind and keep learning.

_____

_____

_____

48

A key piece of advice I wish I received earlier in my career was to find a mentor. Finding a good mentor is important for successful development as a leader. Do you have a mentor?

_____

_____

_____

49

What does your circle of associates look like? Great leaders know they need diversity of thought to excel. Diversify your circle of associates early in your career to maximize your leadership capacity and chances of success.

_____

_____

_____

50

Organizations have a Board of Directors to help guide their decision making. Do you have a personal Board of Directors to help guide you in your decision making?

_____

_____

_____

51

Learn to bloom where you have
been planted. —Daniel Sydlik

_____

_____

_____

Share the AHA messages from this book socially by going to
http://aha.pub/EmergingLeaders.

Section III

Leadership Development of Self

Great leaders have a high level of emotional intelligence. As a result, they know themselves well and how to control themselves rather than be slaves to their impulses. Instead of allowing their impulses to go unchecked, they redirect them in ways that are healthy and meaningful.

Knowing oneself as a leader includes having an awareness of strengths and weaknesses. Developing oneself as a leader involves shoring up strengths so they remain strengths rather than atrophy and become weaknesses. Leadership development of self also includes working on weaknesses and striving to be a well-rounded leader.

Emerging leaders do well to invest in themselves early and often. This means looking for educational opportunities to learn and gain new credibility, credentials, and certifications every year. This means looking for annual opportunities to gain transformational life experiences through travel to places across the globe, where they can expand their understanding of other cultures and places.

Developing oneself as a leader is one of the greatest investments of time, money, and resources an emerging leader can make. Budget the time and money to buy these experiences that, unlike material possessions, can never be taken away and will continue to pay dividends throughout one's life.

52

Leadership Development is similar to being on an airplane: before we can save someone else, we must first save ourselves. What are you doing to develop yourself as a leader?

_____

_____

_____

53

Lead without authority. Influence without power!

_____

_____

_____

54

"Lead by example!" These simple words our parents taught us don't just apply to our external actions but also our internal actions. To lead myself externally (actions), I must first lead myself internally (thoughts). How are you leading?

_____

_____

_____

55

Developing ourselves as leaders does not need to be an expensive endeavor. There are many free or low-cost options available, including online college courses, online videos, and articles. What resources are you using to develop as a leader?

56

Not all readers are leaders, but all leaders are readers.
—Harry Truman
How much time do you allocate for reading each day?

_____

_____

_____

57

Leadership and learning are indispensable to each other.
—John F. Kennedy

_____

_____

_____

58

It is difficult to lead if we are not actively filling ourselves with new knowledge. We live in the information age, where access to knowledge has increased exponentially. Are you taking advantage of this as a leader?

_____

_____

_____

59

It's more important to be INTERESTED than INTERESTING!
—Jane Fonda
Everyone has a story. Are you more interested in others than yourself?

_____

_____

_____

60

Part of developing oneself as a leader is about giving ourselves to others. Great leaders find a cause to donate their time, energy, and resources to help others. What charitable organizations do you support?

_____

_____

_____

61

Marshall Goldsmith's book, "What Got You Here, Won't Get You There!" should be required reading for all emerging leaders. Effective leaders don't rely on the same methods and strategies throughout their career. Constantly retool and retrain!

_____

_____

_____

62

Great leaders know it is best not to judge others. For one, we rarely have all the facts. Also, in time, we might find ourselves guilty of the same thing we are condemning others for. No one likes a hypocrite. Be slow about judging.

_____

_____

_____

63

A SETBACK is a SETUP for a COMEBACK!
—Dr. Willie Jolley
Great leaders understand failure is part of growing,
and therefore, they are resilient. How resilient are you?

_____

_____

_____

64

Great leaders know the sun will not always shine.
They also know the skies will not always be cloudy.
Nothing last forever. Everything is temporary.
Weather the storms of life with a positive attitude.

_____

_____

_____

65

Great leaders don't procrastinate. Great leaders seize
the moment, realizing tomorrow is not promised.
Things change quickly.

_____

_____

_____

66

Done is better than perfect.
Imperfect is better than not at all!
—Tim Durkin

67

Invest in brand YOU! Build your personal brand
and knowledge base by seeking new professional
development experiences every year.

68

Join the professional association that represents the profession you work in to accelerate your growth and build your network. —Dr. Rob Pennington

_____

_____

_____

69

Great leaders know what kids on playgrounds quickly
figure out: you get better, faster, and stronger by
playing with kids better, faster, and stronger.
—Dr. Ronald Heifetz
The same principle applies
to leadership development.

_____

_____

_____

70

If a mechanic shakes your clean hand with his dirty hand, your clean hand won't make his dirty hand clean. The dirt rubs off on you! The same is true with your associates. Great leaders choose their associates wisely, so good habits rub off on them.

_____

_____

_____

71

You are the sum of your five closest associates.
—Walter Bond
Do you like how that adds up?

_____

_____

_____

72

To develop yourself as a leader, you must continuously set goals. When is the last time you set a goal? Take a moment. Think about it. Set a goal for something you would like to achieve and write it down now.

_____

_____

_____

73

The best way to cement learning in your own mind is to teach someone else. The next time you learn something meaningful, try audibly sharing it with at least three people and notice how much your rate of retention increases.

_____

_____

_____

74

The Biblical words: "There is more happiness in giving than there is in receiving," nicely apply to leadership development. When we give of ourselves to develop others, we simultaneously develop ourselves.

_____

_____

_____

75

Builders have a choice in materials when building a structure. What type of structure are you? Are you able to handle the fiery heat and blistering storms of life, or do you quickly fall apart? Build yourself into a leader who endures over time.

_____

_____

_____

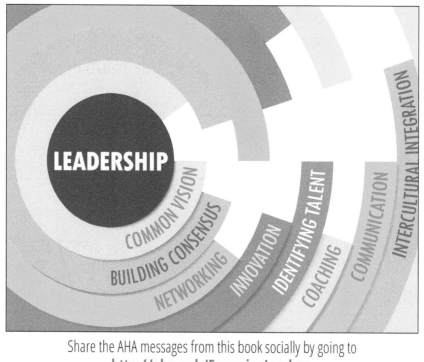

Share the AHA messages from this book socially by going to
http://aha.pub/EmergingLeaders.

Section IV

Leadership Development of Others

True leadership is not about a title or a position of authority. True leadership is not about how well we control others, but rather how well we help others grow into their own role as a leader. This involves being interested in others as unique individuals and helping them develop their own unique capacity as a leader.

Helping others develop as a leader is one of the greatest legacies a leader can leave in their home, place of employment, place of worship, and the community in which they reside. We can help develop leaders through our formal work inside organizations. We can help through our volunteer work in community organizations. We can help through coaching school events in the community and by participating in mentoring programs offered through schools and civic organizations.

There are innumerable ways to help others develop as emerging leaders. Emerging leaders recognize the value in helping others. They're not only doing the right thing, they're also helping themselves.

76

One of the best investments a leader can make
is to develop other people as leaders.
Do you invest in others?

_____

_____

_____

77

Sometimes you have to believe in people until they
have enough confidence to believe in themselves.
—Dr. Willie Jolley

_____

_____

_____

78

I spent most of my early years as a trainer and a consultant. When I began coaching, I had to learn the difference between coaching, training, and consulting. Understanding the difference helps when deciding what to do to develop others.

_____

_____

_____

79

As a coach, I'm an expert in the process, not the content. My job is to use the process to extract the content and solutions from the client to help develop them into the best version of themselves and achieve their goals and dreams.

_____

_____

_____

80

Contrary to popular belief, coaches do not need to have performed the job of a client to know how to help them improve performance and be effective.

_____

_____

_____

81

Giving someone our undivided attention is one of the best gifts we can give them in today's hyper-stimulated technological world. To help develop others, live in the moment. Be fully present.

_____

_____

_____

82

One of the best ways to develop people is to trust them and give them a chance. Sometimes, people don't develop—not because they don't have the ability, but because they never had someone believe in them enough to give them a chance.

_____

_____

_____

83

Leadership assessments such as EQ-i and The Leadership Circle Profile help leaders discover their strengths and identify their weaknesses. These instruments are integral to leadership development.

_____

_____

_____

84

HURT people, HURT people! —Unknown
Great leaders manage their own emotions
rather than lash out at others.

_____

_____

_____

85

Great leaders understand the power of long-term
thinking. Avoid short-sightedness.
Develop the capacity to think deeply and broadly.
This will have a positive effect on decision making.

_____

_____

_____

86

All managers should be coaches first and managers second. Provide coaching to people on your team to help them maximize their performance and develop as leaders. Invest in professionally certified coaches when possible.

_____

_____

_____

87

Great facilitators tap the collective intelligence of groups by making sure every voice is heard. Leaders likewise understand that listening to people and dignifying them as intelligent and having value inspires confidence and develops others.

_____

_____

_____

88

All change should be to lead an organization to a higher level. Be the Change, Lead the Change!

_____

_____

_____

89

Great leaders understand emerging leaders want to work with people as talented as they are. Like a sports team, leaders should constantly assess the performance of their teams and upgrade regularly.

_____

_____

_____

90

What you think about, you bring about!
—Brian Tracy
Leaders feed their minds positive thoughts and have clearly defined goals they think about constantly.

_____

_____

_____

91

We help develop others when we are honest and candid. Leaders have to be prepared to have difficult conversations.

_____

_____

_____

92

You don't have to be great to start,
but you have to start to be great.
—Zig Ziglar
Great leaders don't procrastinate. Do you?

_____

_____

_____

93

Help others develop by helping them set goals. Hold
them accountable by encouraging them to write in a
daily journal. Challenge them to do things outside their
comfort zone. Have them explain the impact.

_____

_____

_____

94

Be not afraid of growing slowly,
be only afraid of standing still.
—Chinese Proverb
Great leaders set goals and understand
you must measure progress, not perfection.

_____

_____

_____

95

Learn how to give constructive feedback.
Some people prefer a good "sandwich."
Formula: Positive words + Constructive feedback +
Positive words. This makes feedback easier to accept.

_____

_____

_____

96

Most of the jobs of the future do not exist yet. When they come online, they will eliminate the need for many of today's jobs. Help others prepare by developing new capacity now!

_____

_____

_____

97

Great leaders are always looking to replace themselves. Do you have a succession plan in place? What are you doing to develop the next leader in your organization?

_____

_____

_____

98

Help others develop by establishing action plans when they join your organization. Don't leave their development to happenstance. Have a plan!

_____

_____

_____

99

Knowing what you know now, what would you say to your younger self? Share this with others
to help them develop.

_____

_____

_____

100

In a world that is increasingly selfish, great leaders can make their mark by being selfless and developing others as leaders.

_____

_____

_____

Share the AHA messages from this book socially by going to
http://aha.pub/EmergingLeaders.

Section V

Living as a Leader

Living as a leader is not just about having a high level of charisma, being well regarded, or having executive presence. To be sure, those qualities are admirable in a leader and go a long way toward leadership effectiveness. Living as a leader involves more. Living as a leader is about providing a sterling example of the behavior others should follow in their pursuit of leadership and success and actively helping develop others to be the best version of themselves. This, of course, will be measured and defined differently depending on the individual.

Emerging leaders recognize early that while few things we do are not often fatal, many things we do are not forgotten. Hence, it is important to be circumspect when making decisions. Decisions we make today can impact us for years to come. People have long memories and the internet has exacerbated this. Our actions can live on indefinitely in infamy or for good.

Living as a leader means understanding that while leadership is situational at times, a true leader is not a taxi cab. A true leader doesn't have an indicator for hire they turn on and off. Rather, a true leader makes leadership part of their very fiber. They are never off but always on, always leading. Leadership is not something great leaders do, it is what they are. Learn everything you can about leadership and then use it to strive to always live as a leader!

101

Every day, we add to the narrative of the story of our life by the way we live. What are you writing in today's chapter?

_____

_____

_____

102

Corporations have a mission, vision, and values to guide them. Do you have a personal mission statement? What is your vision for your life? What values guide you in your decision making?

_____

_____

_____

103

A friend once told me: I've never had a problem that an hour of reading and a good night's rest didn't solve. What's your panacea?

104

Work with a sense of urgency! Avoid complacency and mediocrity. Never take it easy. The best athletes train in the summer while their competition is on vacation. Be a great corporate athlete!

105

Leaders must be well-rounded and avoid being myopic.

_____

_____

_____

106

Never underestimate the power of kindness. As the saying goes, "It's nice to be important but it's more important to be nice."

_____

_____

_____

109

Reputations are made or lost during times of crisis. The role of the leader in times of crisis is to define reality and give hope. —Kenneth Chenault

---

110

There is no softer pillow than a good conscience. —Unknown

How do the decisions you make leave you feeling at the end of the day?

107

When you need to innovate, you need collaboration.
—Marissa Mayer
Do you know how to collaborate?

_____

_____

_____

108

Confidentiality is important. The higher you go in your career, the more you will handle sensitive information. Violations ruin relationships, reputations, careers, and organizations. —Ashlea Turner

_____

_____

_____

111

Every time you have to speak, you are auditioning
for leadership! —James Humes
Our effectiveness as a speaker
says a lot about us as a leader.

_____

_____

_____

112

Many people are successful today because one person
believed they could be successful. Be that person for
someone. Speak life into their career. Tell them they
can and show them how. —Ashlea Turner

_____

_____

_____

113

How do you get what you want? Don't be shy!
Sometimes the only reason you don't get something is
because you did not ask for it. "Ask Outrageously!"
—Linda Swindling

114

Don't stumble over something BEHIND you!
Great leaders look ahead and don't
waste energy on "what could have been."

115

Never be too proud or too busy to help someone in their career. You might be the difference between their struggle and their miracle. —Ashlea Turner

_____

_____

_____

116

"You Are a Brand!" —Catherine Kaputa
Are you building your brand?

_____

_____

_____

117

Do you repel or do you attract? Why should someone be drawn to you? What is your drawing card? What is your brand? —Michael Bernard Thomas

_____

_____

_____

118

A friend once said: "The best inheritance a father can leave his children is a good example." What example are you leaving as a parent and/or as a leader?

_____

_____

_____

119

Be the boss you always wish you had. —Lance Long

_____

_____

_____

120

Many good people have failed because they had their wishbone where there backbone should have been.
—Unknown
Do you wish and hope, or do you make things happen?
Do you stand for something, or do you allow others to bend you to their will?

_____

_____

_____

121

I skate to where the puck is going to be,
not where it's been!
—Wayne Gretsky
As a leader, have you learned to
anticipate needs and trends?

_____

_____

_____

122

If your actions inspire others to dream more, learn
more, do more, and become more, you are a leader.
—John Quincy Adams

_____

_____

_____

123

As a leader, you operate without a framework at your own peril! Without a framework, you are shooting from the hip and winging it! —Dr. Ronald Heifetz
What frameworks do you use as a leader?

_____

_____

_____

124

There is a difference between your IQ and your EQ. People with a high intelligence quotient can be successful. Growing evidence suggests the most effective leaders have a high emotional quotient.
Are you emotionally intelligent?

_____

_____

_____

125

"Your smile is your logo. Your personality is your business card. How you leave people feeling after an experience with you is your trademark."—Jay Danzie

_____

_____

_____

126

"Manage Your Energy Not Your Time"
—Harvard Business Review
Getting enough sleep and exercise combined with a good diet gives us more energy to be more efficient with less time.

_____

_____

_____

127

Great leaders realize the biggest measurement of their success as a leader is the number of leaders they produce and the legacy they leave. How are you measuring up?

_____

_____

_____

128

Public speaking is a great way to position yourself as a leader. Look for speaking opportunities and speak as often as you can.

_____

_____

_____

129

Leaders take time for reflective meditation on the deep things of life and where they are in the grand scheme of things. Do you practice meditation and reflection?

_____

_____

_____

130

Living as a leader means having your voice heard. Try blogging, speaking at conferences, or getting interviewed on podcasts to give others access to your thought leadership.

_____

_____

_____

131

Leaders take ownership of their careers and don't wait for their boss, HR, or someone else to do the planning for them. What are you doing to advance your career today?

_____

_____

_____

132

Living as a leader means setting the example in how to handle both good and bad circumstances. Anyone can be nice under ideal circumstances. It's how we handle difficult times and difficult people that shows the type of leader we are.

_____

_____

_____

133

Are you where you want to be as a leader? If not, what are you doing about it? It's never too late to become the leader you want to be. Invest in a professionally certified coach.

_____

_____

_____

134

Every great athlete has a coach. We all need an independent person to look at us objectively and help identify blind spots. Great leaders who want to be great corporate athletes invest in coaching to develop and maintain a competitive edge.

_____

_____

_____

135

To achieve big things in business, you need a great mentor and a good coach. You also need a sponsor. Sponsors open doors and allow you to make sustained transformational changes in a business. Do you have a sponsor?

_____

_____

_____

136

Invest in your network! What have you done to help someone in your network lately? When is the last time you communicated with one of your connections on LinkedIn? Don't let your connections get stale. Networking is the lifeblood of business.

_____

_____

_____

137

How you do your job defines you. Are you happy with what your work says about you?

_____

_____

_____

138

Living as a leader means understanding your digital footprint matters. What does your online presence say about you? What do others say about you online?
—Sylvie di Giusto

_____

_____

_____

139

It's not about WHO you know ...
It's about who knows YOU!
—Tim Durkin

_____

_____

_____

140

Being an emerging leader does not mean you are not
already a leader. You are a leader! You have potential
for even greater leadership capacity! Keep developing!
Keep growing! Keep emerging!

_____

_____

_____

Conclusion

The world is starving for good leadership. As an emerging leader, it is my sincere hope you will consider the ideas in this short, actionable leadership journal to develop your leadership capacity and answer the call to provide the leadership our world needs.

As I learned from Dr. Ronald Heitfetz, leadership is an art and is about action. It is not a science that is prescriptive. One must learn the different nuances of leadership as it applies in various circumstances.

There are numerous theories to select as an operating guide. I encourage you to explore the different leadership theories available. Select one or two and make them your own. Whatever leadership theory you choose to live by, it is important to realize it is an art form that must be practiced to gain competency. Once competent, more practice is needed to maintain that competency. In the same manner physicians refer to their work as a practice, so should leadership practitioners. We will never master leadership fully, but we can certainly continue to learn, apply, and develop as much as we possibly can.

True leadership is not like a garment we put on and take off. Leadership must be exercised in every aspect of our lives and in all our actions. May others benefit as you continue your emergence and development as a leader! I wish you success on your journey.

Eddie Turner Jr.

Appendix A

What is an Emerging Leader?

When I decided to write this book for emerging leaders, I interviewed people to learn how others understand the phrase, "emerging leader." I asked a random sample of individuals the simple question: "What is an emerging leader?" It was quite illuminating to hear the various interpretations.

The most popular response was that an emerging leader is a high-performing employee in a corporation who shows great promise as a leader. Perhaps the next most popular response was that an emerging leader is a young person who shows leadership potential.

Those definitions are certainly accurate. However, there were other definitions I heard and others I have experienced in my corporate career. Individuals who are fresh out of college, those early in their career, and even students are emerging leaders. Also, there is increasingly a new class of employee who transitions into a completely different career than the one they started in. They may not fit the traditional definition, but they, too, are an emerging leader. Finally, we might say that anyone embarking on a leadership opportunity is an emerging leader.

Because there are several interpretations of what defines an emerging leader, I believe it is important to expand our traditional lens. Let's examine each word independently.

Emerge

Merriam Webster provides a simple definition of *emerge*. It means to *"become known"* or to *"come into view."* That definition is quite fitting in our examination of what it means to be an emerging leader. If we look at it as *"becoming known"* as a leader, that means it is far more applicable than the traditional definition. With this expanded lens, the opportunity is open for many more people to *"come into view"* as a leader in the eyes of others.

Leader

What does it mean to be a leader? Many definitions exist. Having followers makes a person a leader. The act of leading. Having a title or position of superiority. These are basic concepts of leadership. Leadership, however, is far more complex than these rudimentary definitions.

What good leadership is, what moral leadership is, what transformational leadership is, and much more needs to be considered when defining leadership at its highest level.

In *Adaptive Leadership*, the work of Dr. Ronald Heifetz, he explores the roles the words *authority* and *influence* play in relation to leadership. Truly emerging leaders recognize the power of influence without authority, position, or title in their quest to become known and seen as a leader to others.

How to Help Emerging Leaders

Coaching is a powerful way to support emerging leaders. Coaching helps emerging leaders develop their leadership potential more fully and faster.

As an executive coach, I have worked with emerging leaders identified as high potentials in their organization to help them accelerate their performance. I enjoy working with these individuals who already have leadership titles but are emerging in a new way.

Over the past year, I have had the tremendous privilege of working as an independent professional leadership coach with a different type of emerging leader: students at Rice University's Doerr Institute for New Leaders. Rice has embarked upon what Founding Managing Director General Tom Kolditz calls, "the most comprehensive leader development initiative at any top-twenty university." Working with these young people—starting as early as eighteen, in some cases, and spanning into the late twenties when working with doctoral graduate students—has affirmed my belief in what an emerging leader is and why the lens must be broader than traditionally held.

Working with the Rice students and seeing the measurement and results show the value of what can happen when you use the power of coaching to bend the arch early in developing emerging leaders. The leadership skills they have acquired are transforming their lives and the lives of those who will be led by them.

In addition to coaching, I believe using a proper assessment tool to help emerging leaders understand themselves is important. In working with leaders, I help them understand the difference between their IQ (intelligence quotient) and their EQ (emotional intelligence). Historically, people were taught it was important to have a high IQ to be a good leader and achieve success. A growing body of research suggests that having a high EQ is a better indicator of good leadership and future success.

I am a certified emotional intelligence practitioner. When working with emerging leaders, I use the EQ-i 2.0® and EQ 360® as my assessment tool of choice to help identify and develop emotional intelligence.

Conclusion
Everyone, not just a select few, has the potential to become known as a leader. Emerging leaders recognize the power of influence without authority, position, or title in their quest to become known as a leader to others.

To help emerging leaders continue their emergence, we must help them continue to develop. One of the best ways to do that is to provide coaching with the use of a proper leadership assessment tool.

The world needs great leaders. Let's do our part to continue to identify, help, and develop new emerging leaders!

Appendix B

What Coaching Is and
Why It Matters for Emerging Leaders

I recently had lunch with a colleague I worked with ten years ago at a major Fortune 50 corporation. After exchanging pleasantries, my colleague quickly got to the point of the lunch meeting. I thought we were simply having a lunch to catch up after not having seen each other for many years. We did catch up, but my colleague revealed that along with the new job that brought him and his wife to Houston were new challenges that revealed gaps in his ability to be an effective leader. His wife suggested he get the help of an executive coach, so he reached out to me.

With that explanation, I posed a question to my colleague. I asked him to tell me how he defined coaching and to share his experience with it. My colleague reluctantly admitted that he really did not know what coaching was in the sense of executive coaching versus sports coaching. I explained what it was and what it was not to my colleague. I concluded by giving examples of why it matters and the benefits of proper coaching.

What Coaching Is Not

Before I explain what coaching is, I would like to explain what coaching is not. The word coach, for many people, conjures up images of sports. From their youth, many people have played sports or attended sporting events at school. Many remember all too well the image of a shouting coach trying to motivate players or persuade an official to make calls favorable for their team.

For others, coach has a different connotation. Some think of a minister, a therapist, or a senior business leader. There are others who may think of a consultant, as they conflate coaching with consulting. As an example, for many years, I ran an independent computer consulting practice where I was paid for my expertise in providing the right answers and solutions for my clients.

Coaching, however, is very different. As a certified coach, I am not paid to provide answers or solutions for my clients. This is different from sports coaching or consulting, where the coach or consultant has more experience and expertise and they are paid to transfer this to the client. In fact, when taking the practical portion of the coaching certification exam, a coach who gives answers to a client fails the exam. As a certified coach, my job is to "teach clients how to fish rather than give them a fish," as the old saying goes.

During the certification process, our trainer would often tell us, "the coach owns the process, the client owns the content." Put another way, "coaching is a PROCESS expertise, not a CONTENT expertise." This was said by master-certified coach and bestselling author Laura Berman Fortgang in a workshop I attended.

What Is Coaching?
So, what is coaching? In his *New York Times* bestselling book, *You Already Know How to Be Great*, Alan Fine defines coaching simply as, "helping others improve their performance." The International Coach Federation, the most recognized certification body in the coaching industry, defines it as "partnering with clients in a thought-provoking and creative process that inspires them to maximize their personal and professional potential."

Early in my corporate career, during my time providing IT support for the financial services arm of General Electric, years before I envisioned myself as a professional coach, I remember the first time I heard the term coaching used in a professional setting. In those days, a coach was only hired as a last resort for someone who was not performing well. It was a secret whispered in the halls of the office. Hence, receiving coaching was considered an act of shame.

Years ago, when I first began working as an IT professional, we used to joke that anyone could call themselves an IT professional. All you had to do is show up and say, "I know how to fix computers!" and you were hired. Then the industry realized experience was not enough. There was a need for formal measurement of qualifications through certification. Now most IT professionals hold some sort of certification to validate their competency.

The same was true for many years in the coaching profession. Anyone who worked in human resources or as a business leader could call themselves a coach. As I experienced in the IT world, that led to various degrees of quality.

Today, things are very different. Organizations such as the International Coach Federation, the International Coaching Community, and the European Mentoring and Coaching Council have raised the bar of the coaching profession by creating global ethics, standards, and certification assessments. As a result, the global awareness of the power of coaching has increased. Effective coaching is recognized as an art and a science. It's now considered a badge of honor! People are proud to say they have a coach! That means their company values them and wants to invest in their development because they view them as part of the company's strategic plans and ultimate success.

Why Coaching Matters for Emerging Leaders

Top professional athletes recognize the need for a coach to stay on top of their game and maintain their edge throughout various stages of their career. "Corporate athletes" also need coaches. Consequently, many senior business leaders, including those in the C-Suite, now use a professional coach to help maintain their competitive edge. A growing body of research shows there is value in not waiting until later in one's career to invest in coaching. Emerging leaders can accelerate their growth and performance by investing early.

Engaging a professional coach facilitates continued investment in oneself and provides an opportunity to having learning brought to a leader in the comfort of their location. Having a coach also provides the leader a sounding board, a confidant, and an advisor to deal with the demands of their career.

Certified professional coaches specialize in life, career, business, leadership, and executive coaching. Professional coaching is different than giving instruction, advice, or sharing expert insights. It's a very rewarding process that transforms individuals and organizations by helping them unlock their own rich potential to create new options and value, leading to improved performance and satisfaction. This powerful tool is important for emerging leaders to know about and use.

About the Author

Eddie Turner, Jr., The Leadership Excelerator™, has been described as "The Consummate Friendly Professional" and has worked for several of the world's "most admired companies" such as Accenture, Apple, Dell, Deloitte, ExxonMobil and GE. He is passionate about working with leaders to "Accelerate Performance and Drive Impact!"™ through the power of coaching, facilitation and speaking.

Eddie is a professional speaker and a national media commentator who holds international certifications as a trainer, facilitator, and coach. He is an alumnus of Northwestern University, where he studied leadership and organization behavior, and of the John F. Kennedy School of Government at Harvard University, where he completed the "Art and Practice of Leadership Development" executive education program. Eddie is now an Adaptive Leadership practitioner and a member of the Adaptive Leadership Network.

AHАthat™

AHАthat makes it easy to share, author, and promote content. There are over 40,000 AHA messages™ by thought leaders from around the world that you can share in seconds for free on Twitter, Facebook, LinkedIn, and Google+.

For those who want to author their own book, we have time-tested proven processes that allow you to write your AHAbook™ of 140 digestible, bite-sized morsels in eight hours or less. Once your content is on AHАthat, you have a customized link that you can use to have your fans/advocates share your content and help you grow your network.

⮑ Start sharing: **https://AHAthat.com**

⮑ Start authoring: **https://AHAthat.com/Author**

Please go directly to this book in AHАthat and share each AHAmessage™ socially at
http://aha.pub/EmergingLeaders.

CPSIA information can be obtained
at www.ICGtesting.com
Printed in the USA
FFHW011920021118
49054150-53337FF